Alex's Field Guides

But Where Do SEA TURTLES Live?

To the great little explorer Arlo Clarke – E.E.

Published in Canada and the U.S. by Kids Can Press Ltd.
25 Dockside Drive, Toronto, ON M5A 0B5

Kids Can Press is a Corus Entertainment Inc. company

www.kidscanpress.com

The artwork in this book was rendered digitally.
The text is set in Pleuf Pro.

Edited by Patricia Ocampo
Designed by Marie Bartholomew

Printed and bound in Buji, Shenzhen, China, in 10/2024 by WKT Company.

CM 25 0 9 8 7 6 5 4 3 2 1

Library and Archives Canada Cataloguing in Publication

Title: But where do sea turtles live? / Elina Ellis.
Names: Ellis, Elina, author, illustrator.
Description: Series statement: Alex's field guides ; 3 | Includes bibliographical references.
Identifiers: Canadiana (print) 20240370449 | Canadiana (ebook) 20240370465 | ISBN 9781525306761 (hardcover) | ISBN 9781525308796 (EPUB)
Subjects: LCSH: Sea turtles – Juvenile literature. | LCSH: Endangered species – Juvenile literature.
Classification: LCC QL666.C536 E45 2025 | DDC j597.92/8 – dc23

Kids Can Press gratefully acknowledges that the land on which our office is located is the traditional territory of many nations, including the Mississaugas of the Credit, the Anishnabeg, the Chippewa, the Haudenosaunee and the Wendat Peoples, and is now home to many diverse First Nations, Inuit and Métis Peoples.

Alex's Field Guides

But Where Do SEA TURTLES Live?

Elina Ellis

Kids Can Press

Hello, my name is Alex, and here are
my friends, the first members of my
Curious Explorers Club.
They want to know everything about sea turtles.

Welcome to your first adventure, mates!

They're lucky I'm here! I am an EXPERT on sea turtles.

My friends are wondering ...

In the sea,
I guess.

Yes,
but where
exactly?

I have an
answer in
my journal!

Where do
sea turtles
live?

I don't
know.

But we are
EXPLORERS,
right? We can explore
and discover the answer
all by ourselves.

Yes! An adventure!

How about
ROCK POOLS?
Sea turtles might love hanging out with starfish and sea urchins in these warm puddles.

Sea turtles are MIGHTY creatures.

Some sea turtles are over 2 m (6.5 ft.) long, weigh over 907 kg (2000 lb.) and live up to **100** years.

Excellent vision in and out of the water

Their internal ears detect vibrations in the water.

Their large and powerful front flippers are used for swimming.

Top shell is called a CARAPACE and is made out of plates

The plates are made of keratin, like our hair and nails.

The color and pattern are perfect for camouflage.

A sea turtle's mouth looks like a beak, with sharp edges and strong jaws.

Their back flippers and tail are used for steering and balance.

AMAZING SWIMMERS

Some sea turtles can

- Swim up to 60 km (37 mi.) in one day. That's like from one end of New York City to the other!

- Dive as deep as 300 m (984 ft.). That's like the length of 3 football fields stuck together.

Can hold their breath underwater for several hours

Their bottom shell is called a PLASTRON. It is flat and protects the belly.

LOGGERHEAD

- Medium-large
- 91-204 kg (200-450 lb.)
- Large head
- Powerful jaws
- Heart-shaped shell

KEMP'S RIDLEY

LEATHERBACK

- Smallest species
- 34-45 kg (75-100 lb.)
- Nests in large groups
- Most endangered

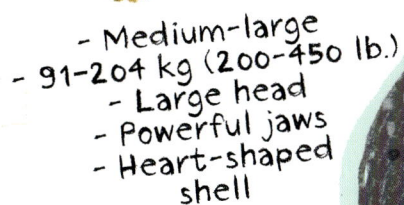

OLIVE RIDLEY

- Small
- 34-45 kg (75-100 lb.)
- Olive-colored shell
- Unique nesting habits
- Great travelers

HAWKSBILL

- Medium
- 45-68 kg (100-150 lb.)
- Hooked beak, like a hawk's
- Beautiful pattern on shell
- Critically endangered

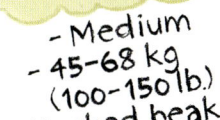

GREEN

- Large
- 136-318 kg (300-700 lb.)
- Herbivorous diet
- Beak has sawlike notches
- Endangered

- Largest species
- 250-907 kg (550-2000 lb.)
- Leathery shell with unique ridges
- Can eat jellyfish

FLATBACK

- Medium
- 75-91 kg (165-200 lb.)
- Relatively flat shell
- Makes flat nests
- Least studied by scientists

ESTUARIES!
Look at all the different
spots to chill.

Nuh-uh. Have you
seen the teeth on those
crocodiles? I bet sea
turtles prefer ...

A SEA TURTLE'S MENU
Yummy Delights of the SEA

Jellyfish

Clams

Sea sponges

Small fish

Shrimp

Seagrasses

Algae

Crabs

Sea cucumbers

Sea turtles have slow metabolisms. They can go for weeks and even **MONTHS** without any food.

Each kind of sea turtle has its favorite treats.

GREEN
Eats only greens like seagrasses and algae

OLIVE RIDLEY
Not very fussy, eating anything from jellyfish to algae

HAWKSBILL
Loves nibbling on tasty sponges, jellyfish and algae

LEATHERBACK
Mouths are adapted to slurp up jellyfish

LOGGERHEAD
Enjoys crabs, shrimp and small fish

FLATBACK
Likes many things, such as seaweed and sea cucumbers

KEMP'S RIDLEY
Feasts on clams, sea urchins, squid and small fish

Sea turtles don't drink water. They get their water from the food they eat.

But because their food is really salty, they "cry out" extra salt through special glands near their eyes.

FOOD WORRIES

Climate change
Increases ocean temperatures and affects food availability

Fishing gear
Traps turtles and also gets eaten

Ocean pollution
Makes food less clean for turtles

Plastic
Confused for food and gets eaten

HATCHLING CHRONICLES
Birth and Beyond

Sea turtles have to travel for hundreds and even thousands of kilometers from feeding areas to nesting areas and back.

This is called **MIGRATION.**

Many sea turtles return to the same beach they were born on to lay their own eggs.

This is called **NESTING.**

Some sea turtles prefer to nest all at once on the same beach. There can be thousands of them!

This is called **ARRIBADA.**

Sea turtles dig their nest in the sand with their flippers.

It is 30-60 cm (12-24 in.) deep.

Some sea turtles can lay over **100** eggs in a single go.

After laying eggs, sea turtles cover them with sand and then return to the ocean to feed and rest.

One sea turtle can nest from 1 to 7 times in one nesting season.

The nesting season can last from a few weeks to a few months.

Because nesting is **EXHAUSTING!**

Sea turtle eggs stay in the sand for up to 2 months.

Little sea turtles hatch all at once.

Baby sea turtles use their temporary **EGG TOOTH** to break through the egg shell.

Hatchlings dash to the ocean, guided by the moon's reflection on the water or the light of the horizon.

Baby sea turtles face MANY DANGERS. Only 1 in 1000 will survive to adulthood.

Foxes

Crabs

Birds

Artificial lights

Obstacles on the beach

Who can eat a baby sea turtle?

Insects

Fish

Beach erosion

What can harm a baby sea turtle?

Fishing nets

Raccoons

Reptiles

Global warming

Pollution and plastic

Seals

So, where DO
sea turtles live?

Well, actually,
almost all of you
are right ...

THE WHOLE WIDE OCEAN
is a sea turtle's home!

Their homes include kelp forests, estuaries, coral reefs, nearshore waters and even deep ocean.

They are always on the move, swimming thousands of kilometers across oceans for food and nesting.

OLIVE RIDLEY

- Found in warm waters of the Pacific, Indian and Atlantic Oceans
- Nests in massive groups on sandy beaches of Costa Rica

LOGGERHEAD

- Found in Atlantic, Pacific and Indian Oceans
- Prefers coastal habitats and coral reefs

PACIFIC OCEAN

KEMP'S RIDLEY

- Inhabits the Gulf of Mexico
- Nests on the Gulf Coast of the United States and Mexico

ATLANTIC OCEAN

LEATHERBACK

- Loves the open and deep ocean, where they hunt for jellyfish
- Migrates all over the world searching for food

Sea turtles are **BRILLIANT NAVIGATORS.** They use Earth's magnetic field and the temperatures of currents to find their way.

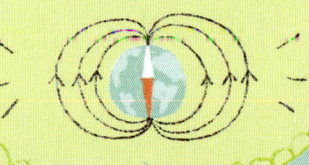

ARCTIC OCEAN

Okay, there are **NO** sea turtles here. It is really way too cold.

Sea turtles usually sleep at night, floating or drifting near the surface of the water.

HAWKSBILL

- Inhabits coral reefs in tropical oceans
- Nests mainly in Seychelles and Indonesia

GREEN

- Prefers seagrass meadows and kelp forests worldwide
- Nests in places such as the Caribbean, Hawaii and Australia

INDIAN OCEAN

While sleeping, one side of the sea turtle's brain stays awake so it doesn't forget to breathe and is aware of danger.

FLATBACK

- Hangs around northern coasts of Australia and New Guinea

SOUTHERN OCEAN

N
W O E
S

How to start your own
CURIOUS EXPLORERS CLUB!

Come up with ideas for awesome club names with your friends.

Plan nature walks to explore parks, beaches or forests.

Organize scavenger hunts to discover plants, animals or interesting objects.

Design a cool logo to represent your club's mission.

ACTIVITIES

NAME AND LOGO

Get creative with arts and crafts and make cool things inspired by nature.

Make badges or stickers with your club's logo for members.

Invite special guests to your school or library to teach you new stuff about nature.

Choose roles for club members, such as the leader, the helper, the storyteller.

Make your own rules, such as being kind to nature and to each other.

Make awesome posters to tell everyone about your club.

Ask your teachers and library staff to help you spread the word.

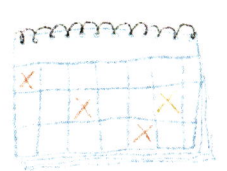

Decide when, where and how often your club would like to meet.

Come up with a plan for adventures you want to have this week, month or year.

RULES AND RESPONSIBILITIES

COMMUNITY

CLUB JOURNAL

Together with parents or teachers, organize a cleanup in your local park.

Come up with cool ideas to raise money to help protect animals and plants.

Make a super-cool journal where you can write and draw about your adventures.

Invite everyone to share their stories in the club journal.

Show your journal to other clubs and groups to inspire them to explore nature, too.

RESOURCES

HOW YOU CAN HELP

The Curious Explorers discover that sea turtles live everywhere the ocean goes (except the Arctic). If we take care of the ocean and the waterways that connect to it, we take care of sea turtles' homes, nests and food. You can help by donating, volunteering or getting involved in other ways. Here are a few organizations who can assist:

- MarineBio Conservation Society (www.marinebio.org)

- Sea Turtle Conservancy (www.conserveturtles.org)

- Sea Turtle Preservation Society (www.seaturtlespacecoast.org)

- World Wildlife Fund (www.worldwildlife.org)

SELECTED SOURCES

∘ Discover Wildlife: www.discoverwildlife.com/animal-facts/marine-animals/sea-turtle-types

∘ National Geographic Kids: www.kids.nationalgeographic.com

∘ NOAA Fisheries: www.fisheries.noaa.gov/species/green-turtle

∘ NOAA National Ocean Service: www.oceanservice.noaa.gov

∘ Sea Turtle Conservancy: www.conserveturtles.org/information-about-sea-turtles-their-habitats-and-threats-to-their-survival

∘ Sea Turtle World: www.seaturtle-world.com

∘ SEE Turtles: www.seeturtles.org/sea-turtle-facts

∘ Smithsonian: www.ocean.si.edu/ocean-life/reptiles/sea-turtles

∘ World Wildlife Fund: www.worldwildlife.org/species/sea-turtle

∘ World Wildlife Fund UK: www.wwf.org.uk/learn/wildlife/marine-turtles